12/03

THE ELEMENTS

Tin

Leon Gray

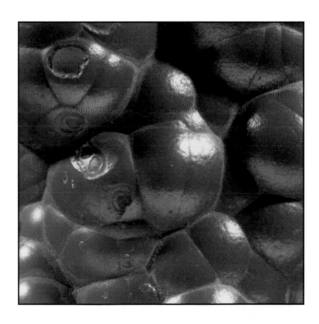

BENCHMARK BOOKS

MARSHALL CAVENDISH

NEW YORK

Benchmark Books
Marshall Cavendish
99 White Plains Road
Tarrytown, New York 10591

www.marshallcavendish.com

Library of Congress Cataloging-in-Publication Data

Gray, Leon.
Tin / Leon Gray.
p.   cm. — (The elements)
Includes index.
Summary: Examines the characteristics, sources, and uses of the element tin,
as well as tin's importance in our lives.
Contents: What is tin? — Special characteristics —
Where tin is found — Tin in history — Mining and dredging —
Mineral to metal — Tin alloys — Tinplate — Tin in industry —
Organotin compounds — Periodic table — Chemical reactions.
ISBN 0-7614-1551-3
1. Tin alloys—Juvenile literature. [1. Tin] I. Title. II.
Elements (Benchmark Books)
TN271.T5G73 2003
620.1'85—dc22   2003052083

Printed in China

Picture credits
Front Cover: Adam Woolfitt/Corbis
Back Cover: Robert Garvey/Corbis

AKG London: 12, Erich Lessing 10, 11
Atlantic Metals & Alloys: 6
Bethlehem Steel: 22
Corbis: James L. Amos 24, Robert Garvey 16, 30, Jeremy Horner 14, David Lees 19, Chris Lisle 15,
José Manuel Sanchis Calvete *i*, 9, Terres Du Sud 27, Adam Woolfitt 4
Getty Images: Richard H. Johnston 18, Jeffrey M. Spielman *iii*, 21
Hemera: 25
Robert Harding: T. Waltham 8
Science & Society Picture Library: Science Museum 13, 20
U.S. Steel Košice: 23
USDA/ARS: Peggy Greb 26

Series created by The Brown Reference Group plc
Designed by Sarah Williams
www.brownreference.com

Contents

What is tin?

Tin is a soft, silvery-white metal that belongs to Group IV of the periodic table. It is part of the carbon group of elements. People have been using tin for thousands of years in the form of an alloy called bronze, which is a mixture of copper and tin. Bronze tools and weapons found in the Middle East and Egypt date from around 3500 B.C.E. Bronze was so important that a period in history called the Bronze Age is named for this alloy.

Tin and its compounds still have many important uses. About one third of all the tin produced by industry is used as tinplate to coat steel food containers. Tin alloys have a wide range of uses. These include solders that join metals together and the bearings of automobile engines. Tin also forms many useful compounds with other elements. Organic (carbon-containing) tin compounds are added to paints and wood preservatives to prevent microorganisms from damaging the material underneath the coating. Other tin compounds are used as pigments and glazes in ceramics and as catalysts in many industrial processes.

The tin atom

Everything you see around you is made up of tiny particles called atoms. Atoms are the building blocks of the elements. They are

Tin is sold in the form of bars called ingots or pigs. These are cast from the refined metal.

too small to see without a powerful microscope. The period at the end of this sentence would cover 250 billion atoms.

Inside each atom are smaller particles called protons, neutrons, and electrons. The protons and neutrons cluster together in the dense nucleus at the center of the atom. The electrons revolve around the nucleus in a series of layers called electron shells.

The number of protons is given by the atomic number. The atomic number of tin is 50, so there are 50 protons in each atom. The number of protons and electrons is always the same, so every tin atom has 50 electrons revolving around the nucleus. Protons have a positive electrical charge, but electrons have a negative charge. The positive and negative charges of these particles balance each other out. This makes the atom electrically neutral.

Neutrons have no charge and are about the same size as protons. One type of tin atom has 62 neutrons in the nucleus, while another has 74 neutrons. Tin atoms with different numbers of neutrons are called isotopes. Other tin isotopes exist but they are radioactive, which means they break up into other elements. The isotopes of tin that contain 62 and 74 neutrons are stable isotopes because they are not radioactive.

TIN

Nucleus

First shell
Second shell
Third shell
Fourth shell
Fifth shell

The number of protons in the nucleus of an atom always matches the number of electrons revolving around the nucleus. Every tin atom has 50 protons and 50 electrons. The electrons revolve around the nucleus in 5 layers called electron shells. There are 2 electrons in the inner shell, 8 in the second shell, 18 in the third shell, 18 in the fourth shell, and 4 in the outer, or valence, shell.

Special characteristics

Tin has some unusual properties. It has one of the lowest melting points of all the metals. Tin melts (turns to liquid) at 449.5 °F (232 °C). It then stays as a liquid until the temperature reaches 4,100 °F (2,270 °C). At this point, the liquid metal vaporizes or turns into a gas. Tin is also light compared to most other metals. One cubic inch of tin weighs about 4 ounces (6.92 g/cm^3). One cubic inch of lead—tin's neighbor in Group IV of the periodic table—weighs 6½ ounces (11.35 g/cm^3).

Tin is soft and malleable, which means it is easily worked into different shapes. It is also ductile, which means it can be drawn into fine wires or threads. Tin is relatively weak, however, so it is often mixed with stronger metals to form a range of alloys with different properties.

Pure tin has a silvery white color. This comes from a thin layer of tin oxide (SnO_2), which forms on the surface when tin reacts with oxygen in the air.

Tin allotropes

Tin is also unusual because it exists in three different forms, called allotropes. Each allotrope differs in density. The way in which the tin atoms are packed together in repeating units to form crystals is also different. Gray, or alpha, tin is a powdery form of the metal. Gray tin is stable below 64 °F (18 °C). White, or beta, tin is the silvery white form of the metal. If you bend a piece of white tin, it makes a squealing noise as the crystals crush against each other. This sound is called a "tin cry." White tin is stable between 64 °F (18 °C) and 322 °F (161 °C). Brittle, or gamma, tin is stable between 322 °F (161 °C) and 449.5 °F (232 °C).

GRAY TIN

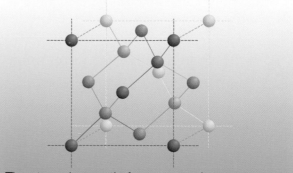

The atoms in gray tin form a crystal structure called a diamond structure, where all three sides of the crystal are equal. This structure is similar to the way carbon atoms pack to form diamonds.

WHITE TIN

The atoms in white tin form a crystal structure called a tetragonal structure, where two sides of the crystal are equal. The tin mineral cassiterite also forms tetragonal crystals.

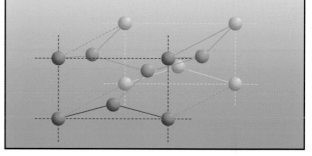

TIN FACTS

- Chemical symbol: Sn
- Atomic number: 50
- Melting point: 449.5 °F (232 °C)
- Boiling point: 4,100 °F (2,270 °C)
- Density: White tin 4⅛ ounces per cubic inch (7.28 g/cm^3) Gray tin 3⅛ ounces per cubic inch (5.75 g/cm^3) Brittle tin 3¾ ounces per cubic inch (6.54 g/cm^3)
- Isotopes: Ten natural isotopes and around twenty-seven artificial isotopes
- Name's origin: The word *tin* may come from the German word *Zinn,* which describes a soft, white metal with a low melting point

BRITTLE TIN

Chemists have not yet worked out the crystal structure for brittle tin. The best way to determine the crystal structure of a substance is to use a technique called X-ray diffraction. When chemists tried to work out the structure of brittle tin using X-ray diffraction, the patterns that indicate the arrangement of atoms in the sample were smeared. Most chemists think that the tin atoms in brittle tin pack together to form a crystal structure called an orthorhombic structure, where all three sides of the crystal are different lengths. The atoms of an allotrope of sulfur also pack together to form an orthorhombic crystal structure.

Where tin is found

All the tin in the universe forms inside giant exploding stars (supernovas) in space. Scientists think that the atoms of heavy elements (such as tin) form as the atoms of lighter elements (such as helium) fuse during nuclear reactions occurring inside the supernovas. When supernovas run out of energy they explode. The blast sprays out the elements all over the universe. Billions of years ago, heavy elements from an exploding supernova eventually reached Earth.

Tin on Earth

Although it is found in greater quantities than precious metals such as gold and platinum, tin is a rare metal on Earth. On average, tin makes up just two parts per million of Earth's crust.

Although grains of native or pure tin are sometimes found, most tin is combined with other elements in the form of minerals. The most important tin mineral is called cassiterite or tinstone (tin oxide; SnO_2). It contains about 80 percent of the metal. Other minerals include stannite (Cu_2FeSnS_4)—a complex tin compound containing copper, iron, and sulfur—and cylindrite ($PbSn_4FeSb_2S_{14}$), which contains sulfur, iron, antimony, and lead.

Women search for cassiterite deposits in a riverbed in the Khammouan province of Laos. Tin prospecting has become a valuable source of income for many people in the developing countries of Southeast Asia.

Tin deposits

Most tin is extracted from directly mining tin ores such as cassiterite. Cassiterite is also associated with the ores of other

TIN FACTS

LEADING PRODUCERS

In 2000, the leading tin mineral producers were

China	64,000 tons (58,050 tonnes)
Indonesia	50,000 tons (45,350 tonnes)
Peru	32,000 tons (29,025 tonnes)
Brazil	13,000 tons (11,800 tonnes)
Bolivia	12,000 tons (10,900 tonnes)
Australia	9,000 tons (8,150 tonnes)
Malaysia	7,000 tons (6,350 tonnes)
Russia	5,000 tons (4,550 tonnes)
Portugal	3,000 tons (2,725 tonnes)
Thailand	3,000 tons (2,725 tonnes)
Rest of the world	2,000 tons (1,800 tonnes)

metals, such as tungsten, so small amounts of tin are recovered as a by-product of these other mining operations.

Over millions of years, the rocks in which the tin minerals are found are worn away by water, wind, and ice. The minerals then wash into rivers and either settle on the riverbeds or move into the sea. The minerals that accumulate in this way are called alluvial deposits. Most tin minerals are found in this form. A smaller amount of tin minerals are found locked away inside rocks deep underground.

Tin producers

Historically, Britain and Spain were major sources of tin minerals. As their supplies were depleted, China, Indonesia, and Malaysia took over as the main sources of tin. Southeast Asia and China now account for more than 60 percent of the world's annual supply of tin minerals. Bolivia, Brazil, and Peru produce around 30 percent. Australia and Russia together supply 7 percent of the total supply. Other mineral-producing countries include Nigeria, Portugal, and Zimbabwe.

Pure cassiterite is a colorless mineral. The dark brown color of this sample indicates that the mineral contains iron impurities.

Tin in history

No one knows for sure when tin was first discovered, but archeologists (people who study the remains of past human life) have found bronze artifacts dating from as early as 3500 B.C.E. This period in history marks the beginning of the Bronze Age. It is unclear exactly how our early ancestors found a way of mixing copper and tin to make bronze. Copper and tin are not usually found in the same places, and alloying metals is a precise skill—the right amount of tin must be added to make a useful alloy. It is likely that copper and tin were already used as pure metals before the Bronze Age. Tin is soft, so someone must have decided to mix it with copper as an experiment.

The history of bronze

Archeologists found the oldest bronze artifacts in the Middle East, but many other civilizations made bronze items. Ancient Egyptian bronzes have been dated to about 3000 B.C.E., while the Chinese were making bronze items such as tools and weapons by about 2500 B.C.E.

Early civilizations quickly became skilled at making bronze and working it into a range of different shapes. However, many did not have access to the tin minerals needed to produce the pure tin.

This bronze sickle and hatchet heads were found at a site near Kfar Monash, Israel. These items were made sometime between 3000 and 2600 B.C.E.

Highly polished bronze mirrors appeared in ancient Egypt as early as 2000 B.C.E. The handle of this mirror has been shaped in the form of Isis—the Egyptian goddess of motherhood and fertility.

Anatolia (present-day Turkey) was a major source of tin at the beginning of the Bronze Age. As nearby sources of tin minerals were used up, people traveled farther away in search of new deposits. Civilizations such as the Phoenicians (a group that lived east of the Mediterranean Sea in present-day Syria) opened up trade partnerships with other civilizations to obtain more minerals. Some cultures even went to war for the minerals.

Around 1200 B.C.E., iron became the primary metal for making weapons and tools. Throughout the Iron Age, bronze was still used to make cooking pots, containers, and ornaments. It later became the main material for bells, coins, and cannons.

Bronze today

Copper and tin still form the basis of the alloy, but many metals are now added to modern bronzes. Adding a small amount of zinc to bronze creates an alloy called gunmetal. This alloy was originally used to make cannons and guns. Phosphorus is also added to bronze to make phosphor bronze, which is used for strong bearings.

DID YOU KNOW?

WHAT'S IN A NAME?

Tin has such a long history that it has been called by many different names. The Romans gave tin the name *plumbum candidum,* or "white lead," to distinguish the metal from lead (*plumbum nigrum,* or "black lead"). The Latin name for tin, *stannum,* comes from the Indo–European word *stagnum,* meaning "dripping," which refers to the low melting point of the metal. The Latin name also gives tin its chemical symbol, Sn. The origins of the English word *tin* are unclear, but it probably comes from *Zinn*—the German word for tin.

Pewter

Another historically important alloy of tin is pewter. A few early Egyptian items made of pewter date back to 1500 B.C.E. Pewter was common by 20 B.C.E., at the height of the Roman Empire. Its use continued well into the Middle Ages. Pewter kettles, cooking pots, cups, and plates were used by

This engraving shows two workers operating a tin smelting furnace in Spain. The worker on the left uses a small hand bellows to fuel the flames, while the worker on the right stokes the fire.

people who could not afford expensive silver items. Early pewter items consisted of equal measures of tin and lead. However, lead reacts with acids in food and drink to form toxic compounds. Modern pewter ware contains the metals antimony and copper instead of lead.

Twentieth-century tin

Until the middle of the twentieth century, one of the main uses of tin was as tinplate. Sheet steel or iron coated with a thin layer of tin was used to make "tin" cans for the food industry. Tinfoil—an alloy made up of 92 percent tin and 8 percent zinc—was also used to wrap cigarettes and sweets.

Tin still has many uses. Recent developments in tin alloys, coatings, and chemistry have led to advances in agriculture, the aerospace industry, telecommunications, and transportation.

DID YOU KNOW?

TIN COATINGS

Tin does not rust, so it is often used to coat and protect metals that will rust. The Romans were the first to coat metal items with tin. They found that food and drink served in copper vessels tasted unpleasant, so they dipped the items in molten tin. The tin formed a thin layer over the vessels, and the food and drink served in them tasted much better. Tinplate was developed in Europe during the Middle Ages. Originally, tinplate was used to make household items such as plates and cups, but it has now found a major use in the food-packaging industry.

Early physicians thought that they could cure diseases by draining blood from the ill patient. The blood was collected in containers such as this pewter bleeding bowl, which is from the late eighteenth century.

Mining and dredging

About 20 percent of the tin deposits on Earth are buried deep underground in narrow strips of rock called veins. The veins are usually found in granite, which is a very hard type of rock. Miners first use explosives to break up the granite to get to the mineral-rich veins. Then the miners dig out the chunks of rock using pneumatic (air-powered) drills. Crushing machines in the mine break down very large chunks into smaller pieces. The mineral-rich rock is then loaded onto a conveyor belt and transported to the surface for processing.

Processing alluvial deposits

The remaining 80 percent of the world's tin supply comes from alluvial deposits in dried-up riverbeds or valleys or on the seafloor. Two main mining methods are used to collect the minerals: gravel pumping and dredging.

In gravel pumping, an earthmoving machine called a dragline scrapes away the debris from the surface of the alluvial deposit. High-pressure water jets are then used to break up the sediments, forming a

Silver ores were once the main quarry at the Cerro Rico mine complex in Potosi, Bolivia. Tin mining began at the beginning of the twentieth century, when the silver ores had been exhausted.

Workers dig out mineral-rich rock deep underground at the Cerro Rico mine complex in Bolivia.

slurry (sediment suspended in water). A gravel pump draws up the slurry into a series of sluice boxes. Each sluice box consists of a channel with a series of raised edges on the bottom. The lighter sediment flows over the edges and out of the sluice boxes as waste. The heavier, tin-rich slurry sinks to the bottom, where it gets trapped behind the raised edges. The slurry is then removed from the box for processing.

Dredging is often used to mine larger alluvial tin deposits. In this process, the entire area above the deposit is flooded with water. A small boat called a dredge then scours the sediment. A continuous chain of buckets digs out and lifts the mineral-rich sediment to the surface. The sediment is then washed onboard the vessel. Gravity separation, which separates the heavy tin minerals from the waste sediment, is used to form the mineral concentrate. This is taken to an onshore processing plant for treatment. In some areas of Southeast Asia, dredging is used to recover tin minerals on the seafloor.

Alluvial deposits are much easier to mine than the underground veins. But even the most productive alluvial deposits yield very little tin minerals. In some cases, 8 tons of ore will yield as little as 2 pounds (1 kilogram) of useful tin minerals.

Mineral to metal

Tin minerals taken from alluvial deposits are fairly pure, but minerals taken from underground mines contain a lot of sulfur and heavy metals. Before these minerals can be converted into tin, some of the impurities in the ore must be removed. Heavy metal impurities can be removed using magnets or electricity. The easiest way to remove sulfur is by roasting the ore in a furnace. Heat burns away the sulfur to produce a fairly clean tin concentrate. A process called smelting is then used to extract the metal from the mineral.

Tin smelting

Tin concentrates consist of tin oxide (SnO_2) and small amounts of impurities left behind after the ore is roasted. Smelting is a chemical process that converts the tin oxide to pure tin. It involves heating the tin oxide with carbon at a temperature of up to 2,500 °F (1,370 °C). Smelting lasts between twelve and fifteen hours. During the process, the carbon reacts with the tin oxide to produce a pool of molten, impure tin and carbon dioxide gas (CO_2). At the end of the smelting, the impure tin is cast into bars ready for the refining stage.

Molten tin is poured into molds to create tin ingots.

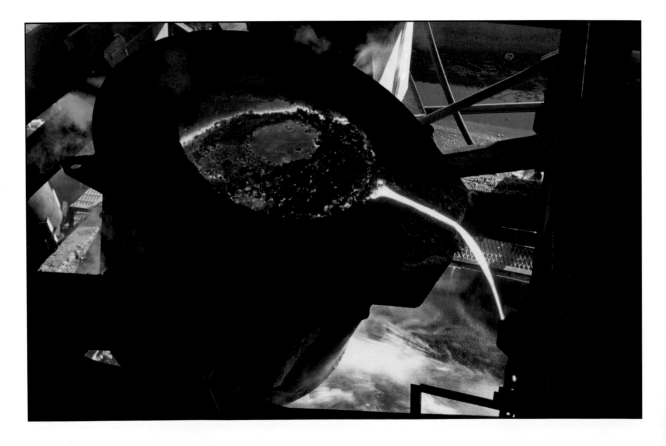

Tin refining

The refining stage produces an extremely high grade of tin (more than 99 percent pure). Fire refining is usually used to purify tin from the smelter. One process, called liquation, involves heating the impure bars from the smelter on a sloping hearth. As the temperature of the furnace approaches 449.5 °F (232 °C), the tin melts and runs down the hearth into a container. Any impurities with a higher melting point than tin are left at the top of the hearth.

Another method is called boiling. It involves heating the impure tin in a vessel until the tin melts. The molten metal is then stirred in the presence of compressed air. Oxygen in the air reacts with any impurities to form oxides. The oxides rise to the surface of the molten tin where they can be skimmed off.

Sometimes electricity is used to refine the impure tin. In this process an electric current is applied between two tin plates immersed in an acid solution. One of the plates (the cathode) is made of high-purity tin. The cathode connects to the negative terminal of the electricity source. The other plate (the anode) is made of the impure tin from the smelter. The anode connects to the positive terminal. Electricity makes tin from the anode dissolve into the acid solution and move toward the cathode. The tin is then deposited onto the cathode as a layer of tin.

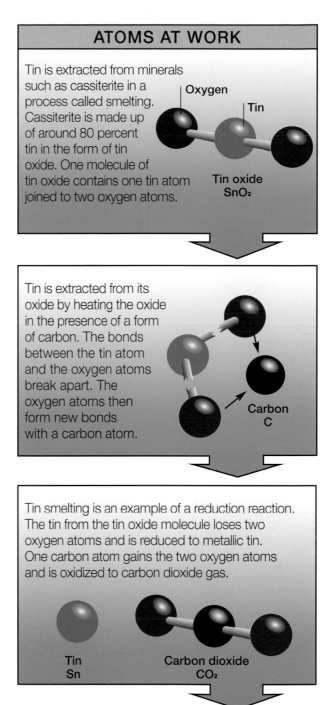

ATOMS AT WORK

Tin is extracted from minerals such as cassiterite in a process called smelting. Cassiterite is made up of around 80 percent tin in the form of tin oxide. One molecule of tin oxide contains one tin atom joined to two oxygen atoms.

Oxygen

Tin

Tin oxide
SnO_2

Tin is extracted from its oxide by heating the oxide in the presence of a form of carbon. The bonds between the tin atom and the oxygen atoms break apart. The oxygen atoms then form new bonds with a carbon atom.

Carbon
C

Tin smelting is an example of a reduction reaction. The tin from the tin oxide molecule loses two oxygen atoms and is reduced to metallic tin. One carbon atom gains the two oxygen atoms and is oxidized to carbon dioxide gas.

Tin
Sn

Carbon dioxide
CO_2

The reaction that takes place is written like this:

$$SnO_2 + C \rightarrow Sn + CO_2$$

This equation tells us that one molecule of tin oxide and one atom of carbon produces one atom of tin and one molecule of carbon dioxide gas.

Tin alloys

Tin is relatively soft and has a very low melting point, so the pure metal does not have many uses. Tin is usually mixed with other metals to make alloys. Traditional tin alloys, such as bronze and pewter, have an important place in history. These alloys are still very useful today. Tin is also a vital ingredient of many other alloys used for bearing metals, metal coatings, dental alloys, and solders.

How alloys work

Metal atoms group together in a uniform arrangement called a crystal lattice. When metals mix to form alloys, the metal that forms most of the alloy is called the parent metal. Other metals added to the alloy are called alloying agents. When metals mix, the atoms of the alloying agents blend in between the crystal lattice of the parent metal. Grainy crystals form where the different atoms mix. These grains give the alloy its special properties. Hard, fine grains are generally stronger than large, soft grains. In alloys where tin is the parent metal, the grains are usually large and soft.

Foundry workers pour molten bronze into a mold. The workers wear protective clothing to shield them from the intense heat of the molten alloy.

Solders and fusible alloys

Like tin, lead has a very low melting point (621.5 °F or 327.5 °C). The melting point of a tin and lead alloy is even lower than the melting points of either tin or lead.

Tin-lead alloys called solders are used to bond metals together. When the solder heats up it starts to melt. The molten solder then cools and solidifies, forming a strong bond between the two metals.

The primary use of solders is in the electronics industry. The solders join electrical components on circuit boards and also conduct electricity through the circuit. Other solders are used to join water pipes together. Solders used for domestic water pipes do not contain lead because there are concerns about lead poisoning. These solders consist of a high proportion of tin alloyed with metals such as antimony or copper.

Fusible alloys are tin alloys that melt at low temperatures. These alloys also contain small amounts of other metals, such as bismuth and cadmium. Adding other metals gives the alloys different properties. Some fusible alloys expand or contract as they cool and solidify after heating. Others melt at specific temperatures. Fusible alloys are often used to make safety thermal fuses. The fuses melt if the temperature rises above a certain level. Other fusible alloys are used to seal double-glazed windows.

An electrician solders electrical connections on a computer circuit board.

Bearing alloys

In 1839, U.S. goldsmith Isaac Babbitt (1799–1862) mixed tin with antimony and copper to make bearings for steam engines. These alloys, now called Babbitt metals, form hard, threadlike grains embedded in a soft, tin-rich matrix.

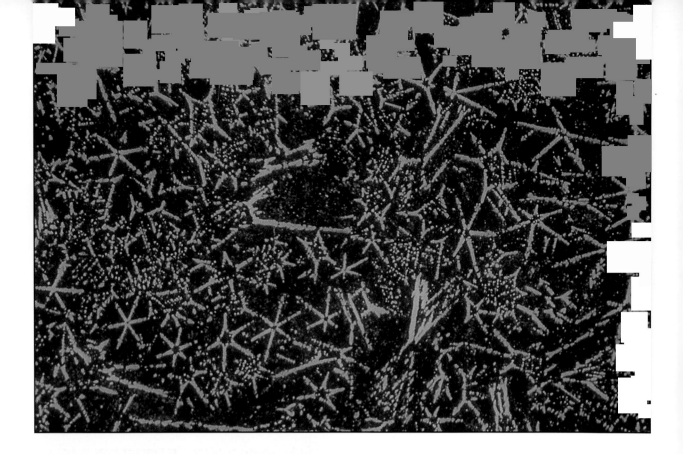

The antimony, copper, and tin atoms in Babbitt metal form hard grains set in a tin-rich matrix. The grains are shown as the white, threadlike structures in this light micrograph.

Bearings made from Babbitt metals are soft, so they can be shaped to fit exactly in the bearing assembly. The bearings also absorb particles that could damage the lining of the assembly. In addition, the bearings attract a film of oil on their surfaces so they run smoothly.

Other tin alloys

Tin forms many other important alloys. Small amounts of tin alloyed with cast iron are used to make the bases of lathes and wear-resistant automobile parts.

Alloys for dental amalgams, which are used as fillings, are made of silver and tin, with smaller amounts of copper and zinc. The tin in the amalgam helps to bond the filling to the surrounding tooth. The addition of tin also lowers the melting point of the resulting alloy.

Tin alloys have some high-tech uses. For example, tin improves the strength of an alloy of aluminum and titanium. This alloy is used in the aerospace industry. Alloys called zircaloys consist of the metal zirconium mixed with a very small amount of tin. Zircaloys are used to cover the fuel elements in nuclear reactors.

Tin and niobium form an alloy that acts as a good superconducting material. At temperatures close to absolute zero (-459 °F or -273 °C), electrons travel freely through superconductors with no electrical resistance. This current might flow forever without losing energy. Scientists are now looking to find superconductors that work at room temperature. If they are successful, it will revolutionize the electrical and electronics industries.

DID YOU KNOW?

WHAT'S IN A CENT?

In 1793, the cent became the first denomination to be minted by the U.S. government. But the metals used to mint this coin have changed over the years. The first cents were minted from pure copper. In 1837, 5 percent tin was added to make bronze cents. This mixture was used until 1857, when the composition changed to an alloy containing 88 percent copper and 12 percent nickel. From 1864 to 1962, the cent was made of bronze containing 95 percent copper and 5 percent tin and zinc. A copper shortage during World War II (1939–1945) prompted the appearance of zinc-plated steel cents for the year 1943. These cents did not contain tin. Tin was also left out of the cents minted in 1962. These coins were made from an alloy of 95 percent copper and 5 percent zinc. The last change came in 1982, when the composition changed to 97.5 percent zinc and 2.5 percent copper.

Tinplate

Tinplate is sheet steel or iron coated with a thin layer of pure tin. By far the biggest use for tinplate is in the manufacture of "tin cans" for the food and drinks industry. The tin coating prevents the acids in the food or drink from corroding the metal below, so the product stays fresher for longer. Tinplate is also used to make containers for cosmetics, detergents, disinfectants, fuels, oils, and paints. The tin does not react with the chemicals in these products. Another use for tinplate is in the manufacture of children's toys and road signs.

Tin cans account for around 90 percent of the world's total consumption of tinplate.

The plating process

Originally, tinplate was made by a hot–dip method in which individual sheets of steel or iron were dipped in a bath of molten tin. Today, the hot-dip method has been replaced by an electrolytic process. In a modern tinning line, a continuous sheet of steel or iron forms the cathode of an electric cell. A bar of tin immersed in an acid solution, called an electrolyte, forms the anode of the cell. When electricity flows through the cell, the tin dissolves in the solution, moves toward the cathode, and coats the sheet with a fine layer of tin about 1 micrometer (one millionth of a meter) thick. As the sheet moves along, the plated section passes out of the solution as the unplated section moves in.

A modern electrolytic tinning line consumes around 2,000 tons (1,900 tonnes) of tin every year.

DID YOU KNOW?

TIN-ALLOY COATINGS

Tin is alloyed with different metals to form a wide range of coatings with specific uses. Tin-copper alloys form decorative coatings ranging from bronze to white. The colors depend on the proportion of copper and tin in the alloy. Tin-nickel coatings resist corrosion and tarnishing. They are used to make scientific equipment and electronic devices. Durable tin-zinc coatings are used to make radiator tanks and many other parts for the automobile industry. Sheet steel coated with an alloy of tin and lead is called terneplate. This material is highly resistant to corrosion, so it is often used as a protective coating for roofing material.

Tin in industry

A geared wheel passes through molten glass. The speed at which the wheel moves through the glass determines how thick the glass sheet will be.

Tin alloys and tinplate account for more than 60 percent of the world's total consumption of tin. But industry relies on tin and its compounds in many other ways. Pure tin helps to make sheets of glass flat. It is also used as tinfoil to wrap drugs and food products. The main use for tin compounds is in the production of tinplate and other coatings. Some are also used as pigments and glazes in the ceramics industry, while others act as catalysts to speed up chemical reactions.

The float-glass process

In 1959, British glassmaker Sir Alastair Pilkington (1920–1995) found a way of making sheets of flat glass by floating the glass on a bath of molten tin. Today, about 90 percent of glass sheet is made using Pilkington's method. It is called the

---

DID YOU KNOW?

RECYCLING TIN

In 2002, around 14,000 tons (12,700 tonnes) of tin was recycled by the United States tin industry. Most comes from tin alloys. This scrap is usually reprocessed directly into new alloys. High-grade (very pure) tin scrap is smelted and refined with the concentrates from tin minerals to produce high-grade tin. Tinplate is another important source of recycled tin. Tin is recovered from tinplate using electricity, producing very pure recycled tin and clean steel scrap.

float-glass process. Glass consists of sand, limestone (calcium carbonate; $CaCO_3$), and soda (sodium bicarbonate; $NaHCO_3$). These materials are mixed and heated to 2,730 °F (1,500 °C) in a furnace, where they melt to form molten glass. The glass is then poured onto a bath of molten tin. Molten glass is very viscous (thick), but the molten tin is very fluid. As a result, the glass flows over the tin surface, forming an even layer. As the bath cools, the glass solidifies so it can be transported to a cooling chamber. The resulting glass is flat and smooth on both sides, so the sheet does not need to be ground or polished.

Tinfoil

In the middle of the twentieth century, cigarettes, sweets, and food products were often wrapped in tinfoil. Toothpaste was packaged in collapsible tubes made from thin sheets of tin. Aluminum foil has now replaced tinfoil for most applications, but tinfoil is still used to wrap some food products. Collapsible tin tubes are also sometimes used as containers for drugs.

Tin compounds

Tin compounds are used in electrolytes during the tin-plating process. Electricity makes the tin in the electrolyte move toward the cathode (the item to be coated). When the tin reaches the cathode, it coats the item with a thin layer of tin.

Glass is often coated with a thin, see-through film of tin oxide. The tin oxide provides a smooth finish that strengthens the glass and prevents it from getting scratched. Thicker films of tin oxide are used to coat car windshields. The film conducts electricity, heats up, and prevents frost forming on the glass. Other tin compounds are used as catalysts in the production of polyurethane foam. This foam is used as padding for seat cushions and other items of furniture.

Tin compounds are used as pigments and glazes in the ceramics industry. They add vibrant colors or glossy finishes to items such as pots and vases.

Organotin compounds

Organic compounds are an important group of chemicals that contain carbon. Every living thing depends on organic compounds. The food we eat consists of organic compounds. Even our bodies are made up of these compounds. In most organic compounds, carbon atoms form bonds with other carbon atoms and with the atoms of elements such as hydrogen. Sometimes the carbon atoms bond with metal atoms. When the carbon atoms bond with tin atoms, they form substances called organotin compounds.

An agricultural worker sprays poinsettia plants with a powerful fungicide. Organotin compounds in the fungicide prevent fungi from damaging the plants.

Uses of organotin compounds

Pure tin and most inorganic tin
compounds (ones that do not contain
carbon) are fairly harmless substances.
Organotin compounds that contain only
one or two tin atoms are also safe to use.
These compounds are added to a plastic
called polyvinyl chloride (PVC), which is
used to make domestic water pipes, food
packaging, and greenhouse coverings. The
organotin compounds act as stabilizers,
keeping the plastic clear and see-through.

By contrast, organotin compounds that
contain three tin atoms are highly toxic.
These compounds are very powerful

*Crops are cultivated in plastic greenhouses in France.
Organotin compounds prevent the polyvinyl chloride
plastic from becoming cloudy in the sunlight.*

biocides—chemical agents used to kill
microorganisms such as bacteria and
fungi. Organotin biocides are added to
paints and wood preservatives. They stop
microorganisms from damaging the
material beneath the preservative or paint
coating. Fungicides and disinfectants used
in hospitals and veterinary surgeries also
contain organotin biocides. Some
organotin compounds are so toxic that
their sale is restricted.

Periodic table

Everything in the universe consists of combinations of substances called elements. Elements consist of tiny atoms, which are too small to see. Atoms are the building blocks of matter.

The character of an atom depends on how many even tinier particles called protons are in its center, or nucleus. An element's atomic number is the same as the number of its protons.

Scientists have found around 110 different elements. About 90 elements occur naturally on Earth. The rest have been made in laboratories.

All the chemical elements are set out on a chart called the periodic table. This lists all the elements in order according to their atomic number.

The elements at the left of the table are metals. Those at the right are nonmetals. Between the metals and the nonmetals are the metalloids, which sometimes act like metals and sometimes like nonmetals.

● On the left of the table are the alkali metals. These elements have just one electron in their outer shells.

● On the right of the periodic table are the noble gases. These elements have full outer shells.

● Elements in the same group have the same number of electrons in their outer shells.

● Elements get more reactive as you go down a group.

● The number of electrons orbiting the nucleus increases down each group.

● The transition metals are in the middle of the table, between Groups II and III.

Group I

Group II

Transition metals

1 H Hydrogen 1								
3 Li Lithium 7	4 Be Beryllium 9							
11 Na Sodium 23	12 Mg Magnesium 24							
19 K Potassium 39	20 Ca Calcium 40	21 Sc Scandium 45	22 Ti Titanium 48	23 V Vanadium 51	24 Cr Chromium 52	25 Mn Manganese 55	26 Fe Iron 56	27 Co Cobalt 59
37 Rb Rubidium 85	38 Sr Strontium 88	39 Y Yttrium 89	40 Zr Zirconium 91	41 Nb Niobium 93	42 Mo Molybdenum 96	43 Tc Technetium (99)	44 Ru Ruthenium 101	45 Rh Rhodium 103
55 Cs Cesium 133	56 Ba Barium 137	71 Lu Lutetium 175	72 Hf Hafnium 179	73 Ta Tantalum 181	74 W Tungsten 184	75 Re Rhenium 186	76 Os Osmium 190	77 Ir Iridium 192
87 Fr Francium 223	88 Ra Radium 226	103 Lr Lawrencium (260)	104 Unq Unnilquadium (261)	105 Unp Unnilpentium (262)	106 Unh Unnilhexium (263)	107 Uns Unnilseptium (?)	108 Uno Unniloctium (?)	109 Une Unnilennium (?)

Lanthanide elements

Actinide elements

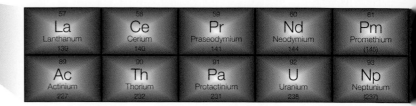

57 La Lanthanum 139	58 Ce Cerium 140	59 Pr Praseodymium 141	60 Nd Neodymium 144	61 Pm Promethium (145)
89 Ac Actinium 227	90 Th Thorium 232	91 Pa Protactinium 231	92 U Uranium 238	93 Np Neptunium (237)

The horizontal rows of the table are called periods. As you go across a period, the atomic number increases by one from each element to the next. The vertical columns are called groups. Elements get heavier as you go down a group. All the elements in a group have the same number of electrons in their outer shells. This means they react in similar ways.

The transition metals fall between Groups II and III. Their electron shells fill up in an unusual way. The lanthanide elements and the actinide elements are set apart from the main table to make it easier to read. All the lanthanide elements and the actinide elements are quite rare.

Tin in the table

Tin is in Group IV of the periodic table. This means that it has four electrons in its outer shell. Tin forms compounds with other elements by losing or sharing these electrons. Tin is unusual because it exists in different forms called allotropes. Antimony, carbon, phosphorus, and sulfur are the only other elements that exist as allotropes.

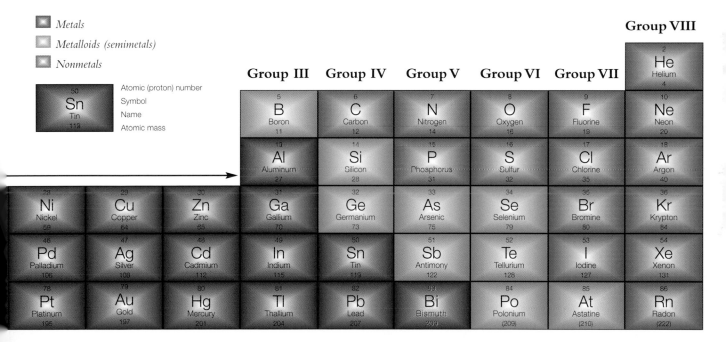

■ Metals
■ Metalloids (semimetals)
■ Nonmetals

50 / Sn / Tin / 119
Atomic (proton) number
Symbol
Name
Atomic mass

Chemical reactions

Chemical reactions are going on all the time—candles burn, nails rust, and food is digested. Some reactions involve just two substances; others many more. But whenever a reaction takes place, at least one substance is changed.

In a chemical reaction, the atoms stay the same. A hydrogen atom remains a hydrogen atom; a tin atom remains a tin atom. But they join up in different combinations to form new molecules.

Writing an equation

Chemical reactions can be described by writing down the atoms and molecules before and after the reaction. Since the atoms stay the same, the number of atoms before will be the same as the number of atoms after. Chemists write the reaction as an equation. This equation shows what happens in the chemical reaction.

Making it balance

When the numbers of each atom on both sides of the equation are equal, the equation is balanced. If the numbers are not equal, something is wrong. The chemist will adjust the number of atoms involved until the equation balances.

A worker checks the machinery at a tin concentration plant in Western Australia.

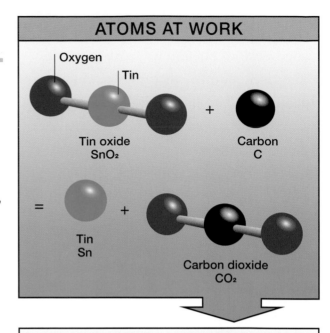

ATOMS AT WORK

Oxygen

Tin

Tin oxide
SnO_2

+

Carbon
C

=

Tin
Sn

+

Carbon dioxide
CO_2

The reaction that takes place when tin oxide reacts with carbon can be written like this:

$$SnO_2 + C \rightarrow Sn + CO_2$$

Glossary

allotropes: Different forms of the same element in which the atoms are arranged in different patterns.

alloy: A mixture of a metal with another element, often another metal.

atom: The smallest part of an element having all the properties of that element. Each atom is less than one millionth of an inch in diameter.

atomic mass: The number of protons and neutrons in an atom.

atomic number: The number of protons in an atom.

bond: The attraction between two atoms or ions that holds them together.

catalyst: Something that makes a chemical reaction occur more quickly.

compound: A substance made of atoms of more than one element. The atoms are held together by chemical bonds.

corrosion: The eating away of a material by reaction with other chemicals, often oxygen and moisture in the air.

crystal: A solid substance in which the atoms are arranged in a regular, three-dimensional pattern.

electrode: A material through which an electrical current flows into, or out of, a liquid electrolyte.

electrolyte: A liquid that electricity can flow through.

electron: A tiny particle with a negative charge. Electrons are found inside atoms, where they move around the nucleus in layers called electron shells.

element: A substance that is made from only one type of atom. Tin belongs to the carbon family of elements in Group IV of the periodic table.

ion: A particle of an element similar to an atom but carrying an additional negative or positive electrical charge.

isotopes: Atoms of an element with the same number of protons and electrons but different numbers of neutrons.

metal: An element on the left-hand side of the periodic table.

mineral: A compound or element as it is found in its natural form on Earth.

molecule: A particle that contains atoms held together by chemical bonds.

neutron: A tiny particle with no electrical charge. Neutrons are found in the nucleus of almost every atom.

nucleus: The dense structure at the center of an atom.

periodic table: A chart containing all the chemical elements laid out in order of their atomic number.

proton: A tiny particle with a positive charge. Protons are found inside the nucleus of an atom.

refining: An industrial process that frees substances, such as metals, from impurities or unwanted material.

Index